TRAIL OF TEARS

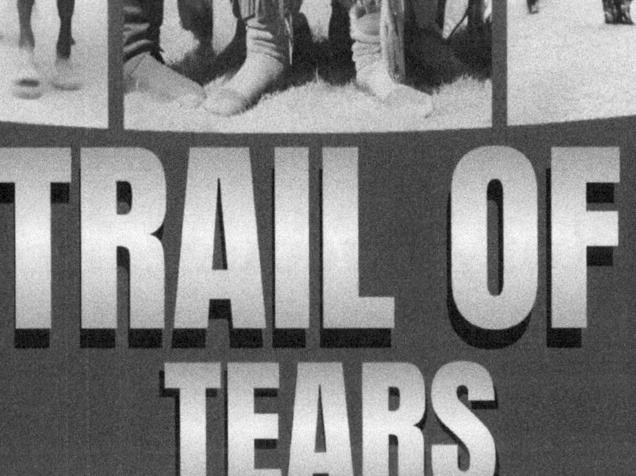

The Trail of Tears: A Look Back At History's Cruelest Acts

HISTORY ENCOUNTERS

History of

Trail of Tears

A Brief History from Beginning to the End

History Encounters

CONTENTS

Bonus Downloads

Want to Fill Your Digital Library for Free?

Every purchase comes with FREE bonus downloads!
Download yours now by clicking the 'Get it Now' button.

Get it Now

Chapter One
Introduction

The history of Native Americans is often not discussed when it concerns the history of the world. Considering that they once covered the entire territory of the United States, it should arouse more concern that they are now a minority in the land they once ruled. The genocide happened differently to different tribes. One of the cruelest genocides of Native Americans happened to the Cherokee tribes when the white settlers wanted to separate the land into white land and Native land. To be honest, they wanted access to the minerals found on land owned by the Native Americans.

At the end of the day, the Cherokees were forced to leave their lands according to unfair or just treaties. The journey from their homeland to the designated Indian lands would kill thousands of their people through disease, weather conditions, fatigue, hunger, and exhaustion. Even though it wasn't technically a war, it was one of the grossest acts of inhumanity in American history. People who had fought in wars found their stomachs churning at the sight of the Cherokee making their way along the Trail of Tears. The dead of the journey were buried in unmarked graves against the tradition and sanctity of the Cherokee culture, but the people along the trail were weak and hungry, having to do what they could to survive and stay strong. The youngest and the elderly were the biggest victims along the way, being the most vulnerable of the group.

One of the white settlers that saw the Native Americans trudging along mentioned that they noticed that every Native American that looked at him looked at him with pure hatred. The Native American tribes were not against the idea of war and pillaging, but there were unspoken rules that they followed. You did not do anything to your opponent that you could not take. If you killed twenty of their people, the enemy was within their right to kill around the same amount of people. It was what kept a certain level of respect among the tribes. But with the white settlers, once there was death in their camps, they wanted to kill all of the Native Americans.

The Native Americans lost their land and all their property, including their possessions. Soldiers forcibly made the Cherokee leave their houses and leave behind everything they owned. Native women who came from affluence were striped and raped along with everyone else, forced into a strenuous journey when they had lived in comparative luxury. The rape of the people was not limited to just women. In order to carry on great acts of cruelty, one has to get rid of any compassion and completely dehumanize the other person. According to the belief system of that time that they claimed was Christian, the Native Americans were cursed, and the white settlers had a right to take their land and rule over them because of that curse.

Nonetheless, the Trail of Tears is a lesson in why even during the present day, there are so many racial tensions and unresolved issues in modern-day America.

Chapter Two

The Cherokee People

"[Those tribes] have neither the intelligence, the industry, the moral habits, nor the desire of improvement... Established in the midst of another and a superior race...they must necessarily yield to the force of circumstances and ere long disappear."

— Andrew Jackson, made as U.S. President at the Fifth Annual Message to Congress, December 3, 1833

The question of who was the worst American president can often lead to many debates, but for the Native Americans, they can almost unilaterally agree that Andrew Jackson, if not the worst, was the most despicable and inhumane of all the presidents. The Cherokee people had long been established in the Americas before the European pioneers settled there.

The Cherokee people had a distinctly different lifestyle from their European counterparts. The most notable thing was probably their higher degree of hygiene. The European Americans bathed sporadically and often didn't bathe for weeks at a time, while the Cherokee made it a part of their routines to bathe at least a few times a week. This is important to note because the Native Americans were often referred to as savages or dirty whilst actually maintaining healthier ablutionary practices than their counterparts.

The Cherokee were quite liberal, and their women enjoyed rights that most women of European or Anglo-Saxon origin could only dream of. The woman chose who she married, and her betrothed would build her a house. If she had too many children or a disabled child she did not want, she had the right to kill it, but if the father did that, he would be judged for murder, and if she wanted a divorce, she simply packed his bags and put it outside the home. The Cherokee women had more freedom and less care, which intrigued many European men. European men had a habit of fetishizing the behavior of non-European women to justify their attraction toward them. They described Cherokee women as having the coquettishness and seduction of a French woman. Their skin was lighter than the other Native American tribes and had smaller features making them closer to the ideal Eurocentric features.

It wasn't surprising then when many of the pioneers copulated with the Cherokee women. The Cherokee, as mentioned by some, was more welcoming of outside men than the other tribes. Their welcoming nature, though, would ultimately bring forth their destruction. Cherokees, even though they were a polite and peaceful tribe, were also proud. Their young men were known, in particular, to engage in violent battles when slit and trying to assert dominance, and they were intelligent. It is thought that the Cherokee were mixed with one of the Lost Tribes of Judah. James Adair, who lived with the Cherokee for more than forty years, concluded that they were because their language and way of doing things were directly in line with many religious observances mentioned in the Torah.

The Cherokees were proud of themselves and their people. They never bowed or nodded their heads at another man but shook their heads. They often referred to the pioneers as "ugly" and said that their features were inferior to their Cherokee features. Even though they were darker than the pioneers, they were lighter than their other Native American counterparts, the Choctaws, the Creeks, and the Iroquois. Despite the condescending attitude, they were still cordial and hospitable.

In 1770, the Cherokees occupied much of the land in what we now know as Kentucky, Virginia, North Carolina, Tennessee, South Carolina, Georgia, Mississippi, and the Appalachian region. Their population was well above ten thousand, and they were well-established. Although the Cherokees had claims on a lot of the land, it was also claimed by other Native American tribes, where oil sometimes broke out into warfare between the tribes. The land was also on the radar of the European settlers. Although the Cherokee fields had no definite borders, they were manned by the Cherokee guards, which meant venturing into whatever they considered there could be a deadly encounter.

At first, the white settlers were not a threat to the Cherokee tribe until things began to escalate. White settlers were moving into land sold to them by members of their tribes, which they viewed as legitimate but the respect didn't last long. The white settlers began to move into unsold land, where the clashes began. They realized that the white settlers had become a bigger threat than their enemy tribes. The white settlers were worse than they thought. War was not uncommon among the Native

American tribes. Still, the settlers did not have the ways of the Native Americans and were willing to use underhanded tactics and dishonorable treaties to get what they wanted.

Chapter Three

How the Cherokee Men Were Reared

When a Cherokee woman was close to giving birth, she would be sent to the shaman's hut, who would chant to ensure that there were no witches that would hinder the birthing process. The process could be frustrating for the new mother as she wouldn't be allowed to breastfeed the baby for a week. The baby would be fed on the shaman's tea so that they couldn't get bewitched.

During the 1700s, the conflicts between Native Americans escalated from inconsequential clashes to full-on wars. This meant that the boys had to be trained for war. Initially, the boys returning from the war came from the Hiwassee side (modern-day Tennessee river) and back much more beaten down and injured than from other places. They would speak of a "white storm," which was composed of white settlers who came with firearms and large numbers and attacked mercilessly.

The white settlers did not have the time-honored war rules of the Cherokee. According to Native American culture, if your enemy killed thirty of your people, you had a right to kill thirty of their people. Still, when a pack of young Native American men killed approximately forty white settlers, the white settlers wanted to wipe their existence off from the Earth. The youth were hotheaded on both sides, and raids happened between the two groups of people habitually.

As time went on, a growing number of the members of the Cherokee tribe could communicate in English but lacked the education to write in it. Then there grew a number of those who learned to write among the tribe, so letters went out to the English settlers telling them that they were the ones that invaded their territory and started conflicts. At first, these communications were heeded, but not for long as, eventually, the settlers would start to kill or capture various members of the Native American men.

As the Cherokee men grew, they began to realize the intention of the settlers. That the settlers did not care to live in harmony with nature or with them for that matter.

"It is true that [great God of Nature] has endowed you with many superior advantages, but he has not created us to be your slaves. We are separate people!" This was a statement that a Native American leader (anon) released as they saw that the settlers were encroaching on their land. He further reiterated their "distinct considerations and circumstances" in terms of their livestock, wherein the settlers had cows, hogs, and sheep while their tribes were blessed with buffaloe, bears, and sheep. While the settler's animals were domesticated, the tribesmen's animals were "wild and demanded not only a larger space for range but art to hunt and kill them." He continued, "They are, nevertheless, as much our property as other animals are yours and ought not to be taken away without our consent or for something equivalent."

The Native Americans heard that the Great War had been lost. The Great War was the term that they used to describe the American Revolution. Because the British had lost, they had lost as well. They had supported the British, who had promised them that they would not invade the lands owned by the tribes and continue to trade with them peacefully. Keeping your word was an integral part of Cherokee culture. The Cherokee had already seen that the white settlers (revolutionaries) were not men of their word or honorable. This loss was a warning for them.

The Cherokee tribes moved further away, and the boys of the tribes often had to rebuild their mother's houses in every new place that they moved to. During this period, a boy built about four houses for his mother due to constant moving. Training for war became vital for all the boys growing up. Besides the spear, arrow, and tomahawk, the boys had to learn how to handle a blowgun. Too many of their numbers had been lost to the blowgun, but if anything, the Great War benefited them by giving them access to guns and how to use them.

Chapter Four

East Africa

East Africa consists of the present countries of Tanzania, Kenya, Uganda, Rwanda, Burundi, the Democratic Republic of Congo, and South Sudan. Djibouti, Eritrea, Ethiopia, and Somalia can also be considered parts of East Africa but are more commonly referred to as the "Horn of Africa." Archeologists believe that the first anatomically modern human beings originated from East Africa. One of the earliest people to be recorded to have lived there were the Khoi-San tribes until the Bantu expanded into East Africa and made contact with the Austronesian and Arabic-speaking settlers. The Arabic settlers spread Islam to the Bantu tribes, but most of the Bantu stuck to their traditional African religions.

The first Europeans to explore East Africa were said to be the Portuguese, who explored what is Kenya and Tanzania today with Vasco de Gama. Portugal wanted to take control of the spice trade from the Arab traders who dominated the area. East Africa became a hotspot for the Scramble for Africa as its ports were useful for trade, and every European country wanted to gain control of them.

East Africa in the modern day is still a major trade route. Many ports are situated there where people from all over Africa go to collect their goods. Tanzania has been a strong port for the transport of Japanese vehicles to various parts of Africa.

Chapter Five

Central Africa

Central Africa consists of the "Central African Republic, Angola, Cameroon, Chad, Equatorial Guinea, Gabon, São Tomé and Príncipe, and Burundi. Cameroon, the Central African Republic, Chad, the Republic of the Congo, Equatorial Guinea, and Gabon) are members of the Economic and Monetary Community of Central Africa," abbreviated as CEMAC. They use a common currency called the Central African Franc, similar to the system established in the European Union with the Euro.

The Sao civilization flourished from the 6th century until the 16th century living by the Chari river. Central Africa would have many empires that dominated during different times, such as the Kanem Empire, Bornu Empire, Shilluk Empire, Baguirmi Empire, Wadai Empire, Lunda Empire, and Kongo Kingdom. During the scramble for Africa, the French and the British would argue over territory until there was an agreement to separate the regions into British West Africa and French West Africa. French West Africa would be what we currently know as Central Africa.

Central Africa is a hub of many activities, and being along the equator also contains some of the greatest riches of Africa, particularly the Democratic Republic of Congo. Unfortunately, Central Africa is often also the home of Ebola. There are many tribes in Central Africa

Chapter Six

The Indian Removal Act: Part 1

The Trail of Tears was a forced migration of the numerous indigenous groups of North America known as the civilized tribes from their ancestral lands in the US Southeast to new territory in Oklahoma. The journey resulted in the deaths of over four thousand Native Americans along the way. On May 28, 1830 thé US President, Andrew Jackson, ratified The Indian Removal Act (a law that gave the American government power to take land that belonged to the Native Americans in the Southeast and also allowed people to make negotiations with the Native Americans to "improve their land", as well as offer resettlement funds) The act was highly controversial. While many Americans, particularly those in the South, supported its passage, many others opposed the act, including a large number of Christian missionaries and several sitting members of congress.

The legislature finally passed the act after a long, bitter series of debates. Its ultimate goal was to turn those lands over to settlers, and The Indian Removal Act did not explicitly grant Jackson permission to remove Native inhabitants forcibly. Nonetheless, the so-called five civilized tribes, which included the Choctaw, Chickasaw, Cherokee, Seminole, and Cherokee, but they also included the Wyandot, Kickapoo, Potawatomi, Shawnee, and Lenape, were all ultimately removed from their lands, and force was often a major factor in achieving that.

The Native Americans are ubiquitously known as Indians among the White population at that time. They weren't terribly popular in any of the states that the Trail of Tears took them through. Therefore at numerous points along the journey, they were forced to go many miles off the main route in order to avoid towns and cities where residents simply did not want them to come through. In some of these places, the landowners would charge them fees to cross over their lands, and not surprisingly; the fees weren't cheap. For example, after traveling through Tennessee and Kentucky, the Cherokee reached Southern Illinois, but they had to cross the Ohio River to get there. The Cherokee were charged $1 a head to cross the river on the ferry, which would be about $23 today. Other users of the ferry, meanwhile, typically paid $0.12 per head, which would be about $3 in today's currency.

A soldier named John. G Burnett, a private in Abraham McClellan's company who was assigned to help translate on the Trail of Tears, recorded his memories of the event on his 80th birthday. In his memoirs, he pulled no punches. Based on his first-hand knowledge, he characterized the Trail of Tears as "the most brutal order in the history of American warfare." While Burnett's recorded memories provide deeply malignant details about the trail, it is his recollections about the brutal weather that he refers to the most. The Natives who walked the trail were indeed forced to face harsh weather. In 1838, for example, the Cherokee were rounded up and put into stockades in Cleveland, Tennessee, until October of that year when they finally began the trail. This means that they had to complete the 1,000-mile journey in the dead of winter. "Many were forced to walk barefoot with only the thinnest blankets for warmth as the sleet and snow fell on them. Due to the cold and exposure, many contracted illnesses like pneumonia, and untold numbers succumbed as a result," Burnett retold.

Bonus Download

Want to Fill Your Digital Library for Free?

Every purchase comes with FREE bonus downloads!
Download yours now by clicking the 'Get it Now' button.

Get it Now

Chapter Seven

The Indian Removal Act: Part 2

After being removed from their ancestral lands and forced by the US government to head to an unknown place to survive, hundreds of sick and dying Native Americans struggled through a desolate land. As they persevered, spectators on the side of the road gathered. These spectators offered no help or relief but often started on in silence, watching for their own interest. The testimony of Samuel Cloud (who was nine at the time), a survivor of the Trail of Tears, had his story recorded by his grandson. Cloud recounts that by the end of the trail, he hated "the white who lined the roads in their woolen clothes that kept them warm watching the Indians pass."

Native Americans weren't the only ones that wound up walking the Trail of Tears. Many of the Cherokees brought their slaves with them as they moved from their homeland in Tennessee to their allotted land in Oklahoma. Many of these slaves were not just tasked with dealing with the incredibly inhospitable conditions of the trail but also had to serve their Cherokee masters as they traveled. They hunted for food, prepared it, washed clothes, cared for the sick, guarded camps, and served as scouts along the trail.

Along the trail, pretty much every essential was in short supply. There was no regular easy access to clothes, shelter, food, medicine, and very little game to supplement the slotted meager and inadequate rations. Many died of starvation along the way. There weren't any coffins to bury the dead in. In addition to this, there was a terrible drought that same year. The first group dispatched on the trail in August 1838 had to return to the base camp (present-day Chattanooga, Tennessee) because the creeks and rivers had dried up. Dehydration also played a large role in killing off the members of the Native American tribes. Private John. Burnett remembers taking part in only one confrontation on the trail. One with a taskmaster who was whipping an elderly man to hurry along into a wagon. The sight of the old and nearly blind man suffering and groaning under the cruelty of the taskmaster was too much for Burnett; having reached his threshold, the private started a fight with the taskmaster in order to defend the old Native man. Burnett sustained an injury to his face in the process. Burnett's account is not the only one of its kind. Conflicts with the taskmasters and the local militias were a constant threat to those that walked the Trail of Tears.

Many accounts included that there was a lack of wagon space available to travelers. Because there weren't enough wagons, only the very young, the very old, the sick, and nursing mothers were allowed to ride in them. The majority of those walking along the trail were forced to do so on foot and without shoes. A spectator from Maine stated that "even ancient females who were ready to drop into the grace were traveling with heavy burdens attached to their back". The route taken, now known as the northern route, went through Kentucky, Tennessee, Missouri, and Arkansas before reaching Oklahoma. The Cherokee anticipated that the route would take two months to complete. Still, due to the terrible traveling conditions, meager rations, and illnesses, the journey took nearly four months to complete. They traveled about nine miles per day. It is estimated that roughly four thousand Cherokees died along the Trail of

Tears. Because of the horrid weather conditions, those who died were buried in shallow graves.

Chapter Eight

The Indian Removal Act: Part 3

The *Indian Removal Act* didn't leave many options for the Seminoles except to either leave or fight a war with a larger and much better armed force. Most of the Seminoles chose to relocate, but not all. The Seminole Indians decided to go to war against the US government rather than be removed from their homeland. When the US army arrived in their homeland in 1835 to enforce *the Indian Removal Act,* they were ambushed by more than a hundred Seminole warriors. In response, the US government spent over $20 million in war expenses battling the Seminoles (showing that they were more willing to spend money to win a war than fairly compensate the Indians). The war left thousands dead and only ended in 1842. The Seminoles were thus forced out of their ancestral lands. Even after losing the war, some Seminoles remained and set up communities in the Florida Everglades.

By the 1840s, tens of thousands of Native Americans had been forcibly relocated to the Indian territories. At the time, the US government swore that settlers would never encroach upon this new Indian territory. As the United States continued its goal of moving progressively westward, the Indian territories got progressively smaller and smaller. By 1907, Oklahoma became the 46th US state, and the Indian state was no more.

"You built your father's house over my mother's grave," Native Blood by Silent Planet would comment on the Trail of Tears. This is the general story of the Trail of Tears that many claims have been whitewashed and made easier to digest for the descendants of the settlers. There are many debates over how many people died, as Native Americans claim that the numbers were much larger than history claims. There is also evidence that the extent to which the Native Americans were impacted is understated as well. In some accounts, there were more than twenty tribes that were affected by the forced removals.

Besides the accounts of Burnett, there were many reports of other people who accompanied the Cherokee and other tribes on the Trail of Tears. One of the most disturbing accounts was that the taskmasters often raped and violated women throughout the journey. Naturally, many of them became pregnant, having to give birth to the children of their oppressors. What happened to these children is not explicitly stated in history. Still, even if they stayed with the Native American tribes, they would eventually have been taken to schools where the settlers would "civilize" them.

Chapter Nine

Forgotten Aspects of the Trail of

Tears: Part 1

George Washington, one of the most respected founding fathers of America, promised to the people that he would solve what they termed at that time as *The Indian Problem.* He was concerned with securing the white settlements regardless of the impact that they had on the Native settlements. It's been said that the white settlers saw the Natives as alien people hogging the land and deserved the land more. Washington entertained the idea that he would try to make Natives as much like white people as possible to make them "easier to live with." One of the ways that he planned to accomplish that was by converting them to Christianity and teaching them to read and speak English.

The settlers wanted to apply their European farming practices and grow cotton. Many Native tribes lived on fertile land, and the number one export at the time for the US was cotton. The settlers wanted to create a unique American existence by erasing the already existing Americans. Zealous over having defeated the British, they wanted to do whatever they wanted with the land with no interruption. The Natives weren't giving up their land easily, and they termed the settlers "squators." A big priority of the US government was to expand and own private property for the white settlers. As a nation, they were trying to build an identity at all costs.

Andrew Jackson would be the one that perpetuated what many of the white settlers wanted to do. Jackson had a reputation for not letting anything stand in the way of what he wanted. His tactic of removing Native Americans from land helped him attain Florida and parts of Alabama and Georgia. He hated Native Americans because his brother was killed by the British during the civil war when the Native Americans had sided with the British. According to Jackson, "the friend of my enemy is my enemy." It wasn't surprising that *the Indian Removal Act* was signed during his first term. Jackson claimed that the act only worked through contracts and treaties. But it has been stated that he knew from the word go that he wanted to kill and reduce the number of Native Americans. The bill said it was voluntary for the Native Americans to move, so they refused to move.

The Natives' refusal to move put Jackson in a hot seat. He set his sights on the Choctaws. The Choctaws were not as hated as the other Native tribes because they had fought alongside the white settlers during the war against the British. The Choctaws signed a deal with the government that offered them a huge chunk of land in Oklahoma in exchange for their land in Mississippi. The Choctaw became the first tribe in 1831 to be kicked off of their land altogether. They made the journey to Oklahoma with absolutely no resources. The Choctaws had been on good terms with the white settlers up until that point. When the other tribes saw how the white settlers treated them, they refused to deal with the US government because if they could do that to their supposed friend, what more than a former enemy?

Chapter Ten

Forgotten Aspects of the Trail of Tears:

Part 2

The Trail of Tears still affects modern-day America. Many cultures, people, and societies were negatively affected in their bid to become the greatest country in the world. The removal of the Native American tribes can be attributed to the trait that America values the most "capitalism". Because the land that the Native Americans were on was increasing in value, the white settlers wanted it for their own wealth. A mirror of modern-day American gentrification.

There is a continued alienation between the Native Americans and modern-day white Americans because of the complete lack of trust. The tribes that were affected by the Trail of Tears were known as "the civilized ones" who abided peacefully with the white settlers. There is sometimes the ideology that native tribes were uncivilized, and fighting was the only way forward, but that wasn't the case. The result is that even in modern America, where it seems that the government is taking steps towards reparations and peace, there is an underlying sentiment that they cannot be trusted. The modern-day Native American reservations are a result of the constant displacement of the people through greed and capitalism. Which has left many of them disadvantaged and suffering up until this day.

It has been speculated that in the modern day, Native people experience more violence, murder, and sexual assault than any other ethnicity of women in the United States. Their murder rate is about ten times higher than any other ethnic group, particularly among women aged between 10-24. The stereotype that Native women are hypersexual and promiscuous is speculated to be a contributing factor to their wanton dehumanization.

Many people protest about the fact that the Trail of Tears is taught as a historical event when during the modern day, the Native Americans are still disadvantaged and displaced. The colonization of the Americas has been so complete that the chance of the tribes ever regaining their rightful and original places is close to nil. There have been attempts to pay reparations for the lands and damage that the early settlers did to the Native Americans. In 1946, America spent more than $ 1 billion on reparations, but that only amounted to about $1000 per Native American. The damage done to Native Americans certainly exceeds that amount per person. Families lost numerous members, vast lands, and dignity. The damage that was done and what was gained by the settlers would easily equal trillions of dollars, but the US government would not be willing to bankrupt its society by doing that.

At the end of the day, the settlers took the Native Americans' land because they believed that they would put it to better use than they did and that the Native Americans were primitive and underdeveloped. Modern times though, have shown that things that the Native Americans believed in, such as living in peace with nature, were actually advanced beyond their years. Unfortunately, there might always be tears as the Natives fight not only for the injustice their ancestors faced but also for the right to dignity and acknowledgment.

Chapter Eleven

Conclusion

The 9/11 terror attack is considered one of the greatest modern-day atrocities of the modern day. Every year people remember the attack on the Twin Towers. The Holocaust was also a great tragedy that people still commemorate and mourn to this day. But there are some tragedies that routinely get swept under the rug, and the descendants of the victims are often told to "move on" and "get over it." Even though historically speaking, one can never know the full extent of what happened accurately, it doesn't take from the impact it has.

The Native Americans are resistant people who, against extreme prejudice, managed to retain their identity and story.

Their genocide is often overlooked in world history and not talked about. Often time even in schools, the story of the genocide of the Native Americans is often glossed over to continue the narrative that America is the greatest country in the world and believes in human rights. The least that the world can do is honor the descendants of the survivors of the Trail of Tears by remembering the story in a way that fully illustrates the tragedy that their people went through.

People in the modern day don't acknowledge that the United States is one of the oldest surviving colonies in the world. The term American is often associated with a white person when the original indigenous people of the lands were of a darker skin tone. Present-day native lands are reduced to reservations that are reminiscent of concentration camps and infertile land. A tactic that colonies in Africa during the colonial period were put under sanctions. An example is when the Southern Rhodesian government forced the local people to move to infertile lands and took prime land for themselves. Humanity cannot progress further when there are double standards for what is considered right and wrong.

Perhaps the injustice against the Native Americans was perpetuated during a time when no one would intervene, which is why it succeeded. The British had lost in the American Revolution or perhaps were unaware of what the white settlers were doing, or perhaps the Native Americans didn't know what to do against the wave of attacks against them triggered by Andrew Jackson. They tried trusting in the US government and its Supreme Court when they were being shortchanged by the federal government and found themselves on the losing end of things even when things were ruled in their favor. The settlers were ready to use any, and every means necessary in order to get what they wanted. Even if that meant killing women and children, using Christianity and pretending to come with Christian values, destroying their crops, and killing off the local Buffalo population to make sure they didn't have food. There was no limit to getting rid of "the Indian problem".

The basis of all this, in the end, was that the settlers didn't want anyone that was not white to have the same rights as they did. Despite Natives being lighter than the black slaves and having hair similar to theirs, the white settlers simply regarded them as primitive and beneath them, even though it was because of the Native Americans that the pioneers were able to survive and settle in the Americas.

Chapter Twelve

"Discuss with Friends and Family"

Discussion Question

Every modern-day country has committed some sort of atrocity, with the USA not being exempt. Some people think that we should just forget about these events and move on. Do you agree with this sentiment? Explain your answer.

Discussion Question

The American government broke every single treaty and promised that it made with Native American tribes. The damages done to the tribes still affect them until modern-day times. Do you think there is a sufficient effort in giving Native Americans reparations for damages done in the past?

Discussion Question

The Native American tribes were often at war with each other. Do you think that these wars over territory are similar to the ones against the white settlers? What makes them different? What makes the takeover of the white settlers more inhumane?

Discussion Question

The sight of the Native Americans on the Trail of Tears was so horrendous that men who had survived and seen people gunned down were shocked. How do you think this was worse than the civil wars that ravaged the territories at the time?

Discussion Question

How would one truly summarize what happened on the Trail of Tears? Was it a great national disaster, a genocide, or a callous act of inhumanity? Explain your description of it and why you believe so.

Discussion Question

What do you think united the eastern and western tribes in the new Indian territory? What factors lead to this? Who are the major players in the unification?

Discussion Question

Gold is a precious mineral that is coveted by many. Its worth could be argued over whether it is worth the conflicts and loss of human life it had caused. Do you think the settlers' greed overshadowed any sense of morality?

Discussion Question

Do you think that Native Americans are still affected by the actions of the past or that people should just move on? Studies have shown that the ramifications of great acts of cruelty can still be seen later. How do you think Native Americans are still affected by the Trail of Tears?

Chapter Thirteen

"Test Your Knowledge"

Quiz Question

1. **True or False:** The members of the Cherokee who decided to stay back in their lands were victims of rape, murder, and pillaging. They were no better off than the members of their tribe that went on the Trail of Tears.

2. **True or False:** The conditions that the Cherokee had to travel in order to reach the designated Indian territories were inhumane, and many of the members of the tribe did not survive falling prey to illnesses such as dysentery and cholera.

3. **True or False:** One can walk the entire Trail of Tears today in commemoration of the original event. Participants need to take a health test before embarking on it.

4. **True or False:** Newborn Cherokees were fed with the tea of the shaman for a few days before they were out of the

mother's breast milk. This was said to keep the curses of the witch away.

5. **True or False:**The American government honored its promise to stay away from the designated Indian territories. Those territories are known as protected states in the modern day.

6. **True or False:** Sitting Bull, the great Native American chief led the Cherokee across the Trail of Tears. His bravery is why he is famous.

7. **True or False**: It is highly suspected that the part of Native American tribes is part of the lost tribes of Israel. This is yet to be genealogically proven, but the basis is that their traditions and belief systems were very similar to the Torah.

8. **True or False:**Significant reparations have been paid to the Native American communities. The reparations has allowed them to recover from the damage done through

the genocide of their tribes through events such as the Trail

of Tears.

Quiz Answer

1. True

2. True

3. False. There is no constant path in the modern day like the original Trail of Tears.

4. True

5. False. The government eventually encroached upon the Indian territories and never kept its promise.

6. False, Sitting Bull was not involved during the Trail of Tears. He led a revolution later against the US government.

7. True

8. False, there has been little done to compensate the Native American community.

References (Works Cited)

1. Weird History, What Life on The Trail of Tears Was Like. YouTube, <https://youtu.be/x54xhAcpS8c>

2. John Ehle, Trail of Tears. Anchor Books

3. Readex, Andrew Jackson and the Trail of Tears: Setting the Record Straight. YouTube, <https://youtu.be/REPRSlkzksk>

4. Michael Johnson, 03 Trail of Tears.YouTube, <https://youtu.be/Sdlx2bT7c6I>

5. Learn Liberty, The Trail of Tears: They Knew it Was Wrong. YouTube, <https://youtu.be/qalhDKLrWEQ>

6. Jabzy, The Last Slave Owners in the US. YouTube, <https://youtu.be/dKxU9C03qCw>

7. A Day in History, A Brief History of the Trail of Tears. YouTube, <https://youtu.be/CM8PcTIRbDk>

Images (License-Free)

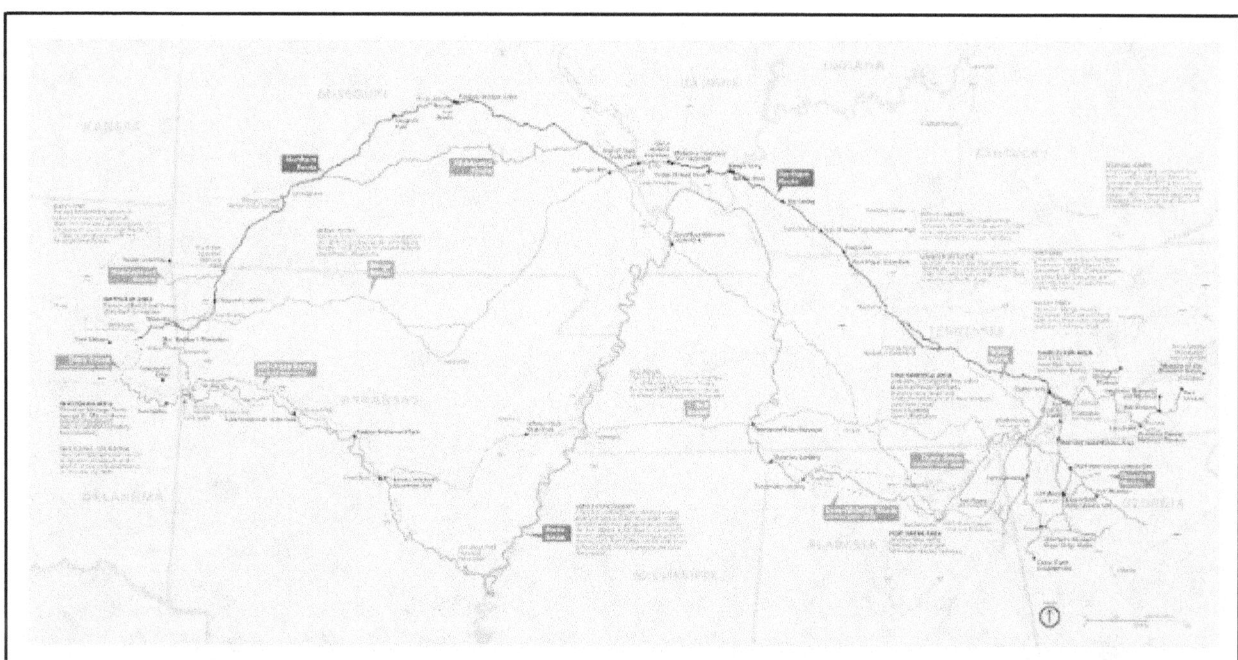

Section 5 Industrialization of Iron, Map of the trail the Native Americans took during the trail of Tears <https://commons.m.wikimedia.org/w/index.php?search=Trail+of+tears&title=Special:MediaSearch&type=image>

Part Four, A painting depicting the helplessness of the people during theTrail of Tears
<https://www.flickr.com/photos/49248728@N00/41717226
3>

Part 1: A grown Native American Man
 <https://www.flickr.com/photos/16943730@N00/48706467413>

Part 2: Very Few People Could be Carried on the Carriages During the Trail of Tears
<https://commons.m.wikimedia.org/wiki/File:Trail_of_Tears_for_the_Creek_People_(7222969326).jpg>

Part 4: Modern Day Sign Leading to the Trail of Tears
<[[File:Trail of tears sign.jpg|Trail_of_tears_sign]]>

Part 2: Elizabeth ``Betsy" Brown was a Cherokee Indian that was on the Trail Of Tears <[[File:Stephens.jpg|Stephens]]>

Part 1: A Modern Day Cherokee Man Contemplating the Trail of Tears
<https://commons.m.wikimedia.org/w/index.php?search=Trail+of+tears&title=Special:MediaSearch&type=image>

Part 4: Museum Depicting a Scene from the Trail of Tears
<https://commons.m.wikimedia.org/w/index.php?search=Trail+of+tears&title=Special:MediaSearch&type=image>

Bonus Download

Want to Fill Your Digital Library for Free?

Every purchase comes with FREE bonus downloads!
Download yours now by clicking the 'Get it Now' button.

Final Words From the Author...

Dear Reader,

It was my utmost privilege performing a deep dive to bringing this book for you today.

Before saying goodbye, I'd like to take opportunity to offer you one final gift. If you've enjoyed this book, may I ask for a small review?

If you do, I'll send you for FREE a most cherished and valuable gift as a way of showing my utmost appreciation:

Bestsellers Top 7 Treasure Box

These are my personal bestsellers sold at bookstores valued at ~$30USD, my gift to you absolutely FREE.

To claim your gift:

1. Leave a review where the book was purchased
2. Send a screenshot to irvinepress@mail.com
3. Receive your gift of **Bestsellers Top 7 Treasure Box**

Sincerely,

History Encounters

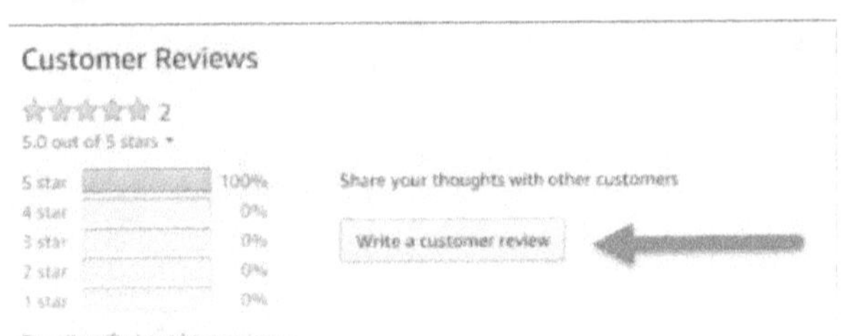

THANK YOU

www.ingramcontent.com/pod-product-compliance
Lightning Source LLC
Chambersburg PA
CBHW080722120726
48001CB00010B/3120